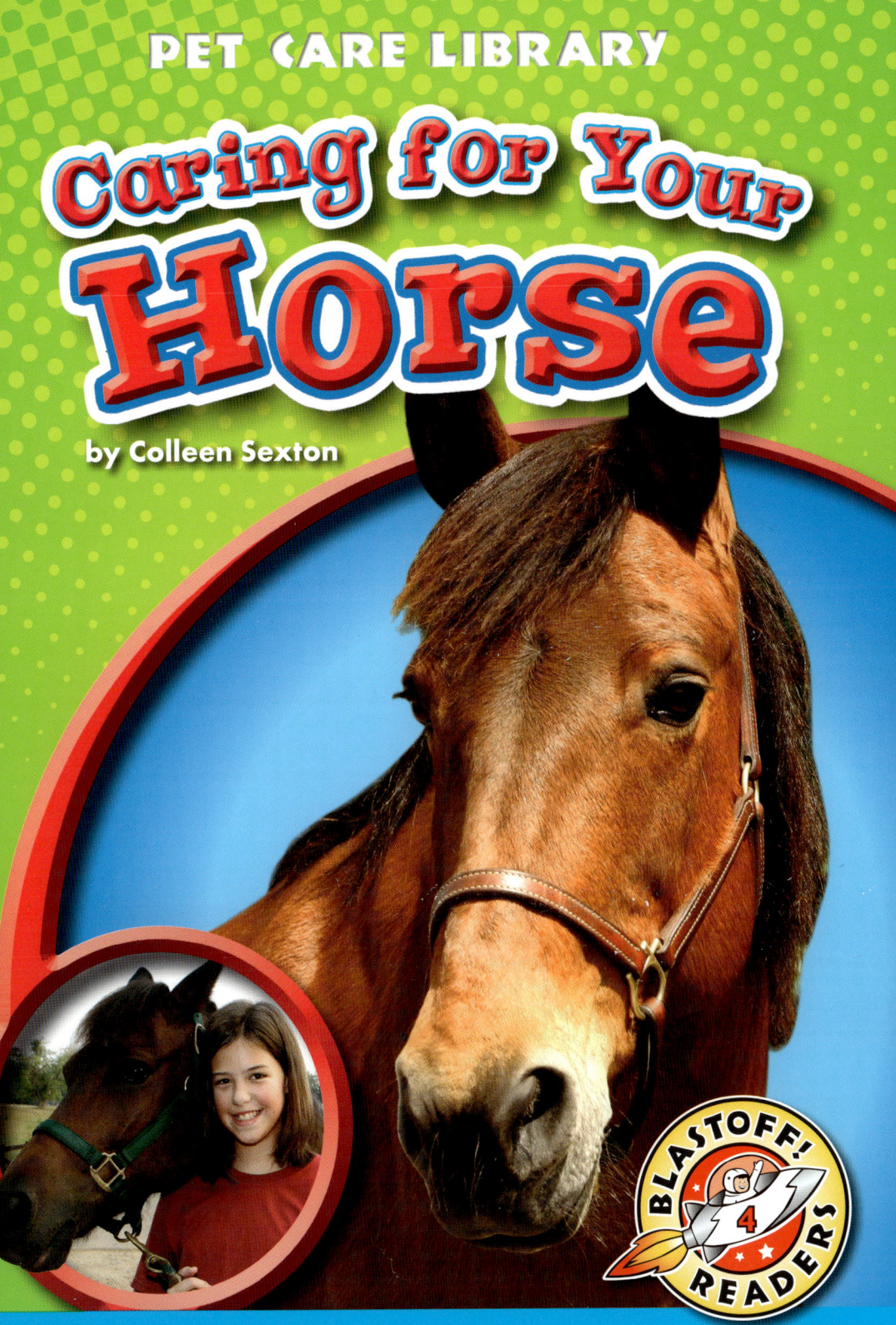

Note to Librarians, Teachers, and Parents:

Blastoff! Readers are carefully developed by literacy experts and combine standards-based content with developmentally appropriate text.

Level 1 provides the most support through repetition of high-frequency words, light text, predictable sentence patterns, and strong visual support.

Level 2 offers early readers a bit more challenge through varied simple sentences, increased text load, and less repetition of high-frequency words.

Level 3 advances early-fluent readers toward fluency through increased text and concept load, less reliance on visuals, longer sentences, and more literary language.

Level 4 builds reading stamina by providing more text per page, increased use of punctuation, greater variation in sentence patterns, and increasingly challenging vocabulary.

Level 5 encourages children to move from "learning to read" to "reading to learn" by providing even more text, varied writing styles, and less familiar topics.

Whichever book is right for your reader, Blastoff! Readers are the perfect books to build confidence and encourage a love of reading that will last a lifetime!

This edition first published in 2011 by Bellwether Media, Inc.

No part of this publication may be reproduced in whole or in part without written permission of the publisher. For information regarding permission, write to Bellwether Media, Inc., Attention: Permissions Department, 5357 Penn Avenue South, Minneapolis, MN 55419.

Library of Congress Cataloging-in-Publication Data
Sexton, Colleen.
Caring for your horse / by Colleen Sexton.
    p. cm. – (Blastoff! readers. Pet care library)
Summary: "Developed by literacy experts for students in grades two through five, this title provides readers with basic information for taking care of horses"–Provided by publisher.
Includes bibliographical references and index.
ISBN 978-1-60014-469-1 (hardcover : alk. paper)
1. Horses–Juvenile literature. I. Title.
SF302.S49 2010
636.1–dc22
                                            2010011409

Text copyright © 2011 by Bellwether Media, Inc. BLASTOFF! READERS and associated logos are trademarks and/or registered trademarks of Bellwether Media, Inc.

Printed in the United States of America, North Mankato, MN.
080110   1162

Contents

Choosing a Horse	4
Your Horse's Home	8
Feeding Your Horse	14
Grooming and Health	16
Exercising Your Horse	20
Glossary	22
To Learn More	23
Index	24

Choosing a Horse

fun fact
People have kept horses for over 6,000 years.

Horses are large, strong animals. They draw crowds at horse shows and races. They work on farms and ranches. Horses can also make great pets!

Owning a horse is expensive and takes time and hard work. Horses live for about 30 years. Your horse will need your attention every day. You will also have to buy supplies in order to keep it healthy.

Supply List

Here is a list of supplies you will need to take care of a horse.

- shelter
- bedding
- horse food
- salt block
- grooming brush
- hoof pick
- horse blanket
- riding gear
- muck shovel
- lead rope

shelter

grooming brush

hoof pick

Appaloosa

Arabian

Cleveland Bay

Horses come in many sizes and colors. There are more than 200 horse **breeds**. You should choose a breed that has a good **temperament** and is well suited for the kind of riding you want to do.

Seek advice from a **horse trainer** or **veterinarian**. They will help you choose the breed that is best for you. They can also recommend where to get the supplies you will need to properly take care of your horse.

Your Horse's Home

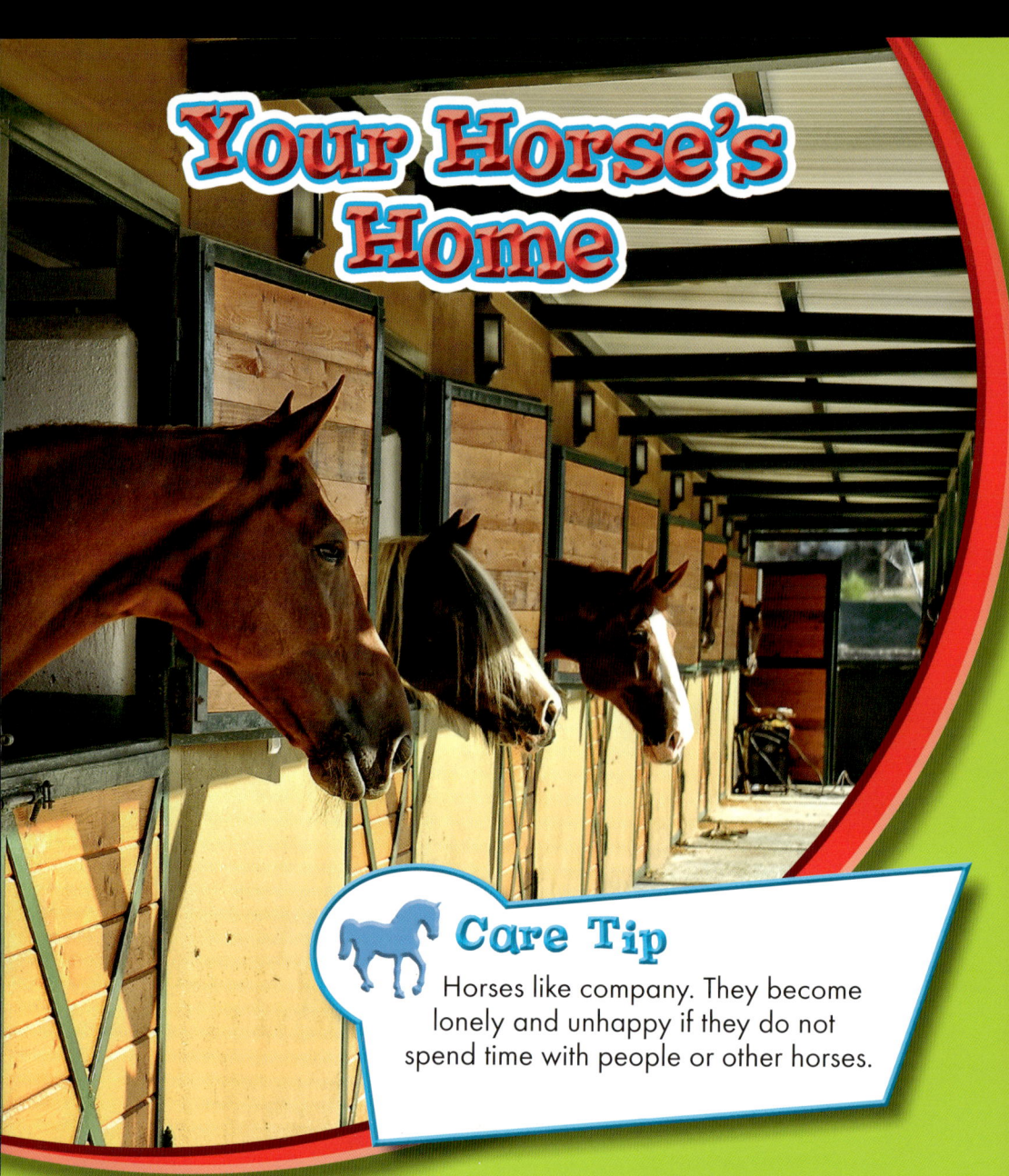

Care Tip
Horses like company. They become lonely and unhappy if they do not spend time with people or other horses.

Your horse will need a place to live. Many people **board** their horses. They pay a **stable** to feed and care for their horses every day.

Some people keep horses on their own land. They have a shed or barn for shelter, an open field for exercise, and room to store all the supplies their horses need.

Care Tip

If you keep your horse indoors, the stall should be at least 12 feet (4 meters) wide and 12 feet (4 meters) long.

A horse can live indoors or outdoors. An indoor horse stays in a **stall** most of the time. The stall should have room for the horse to move around.

An outdoor horse roams in a fenced-in **pasture**. It needs protection from the weather. Both sheds and barns provide good shelter.

Your horse needs **bedding** to rest on. Put a layer of sawdust, straw, or wood shavings on the floor of the stall or shelter. The bedding should be at least 8 inches (20 centimeters) thick.

Muck the stall or shelter at least once a day. Scoop out **manure**. Remove soiled bedding and replace it with fresh, clean bedding.

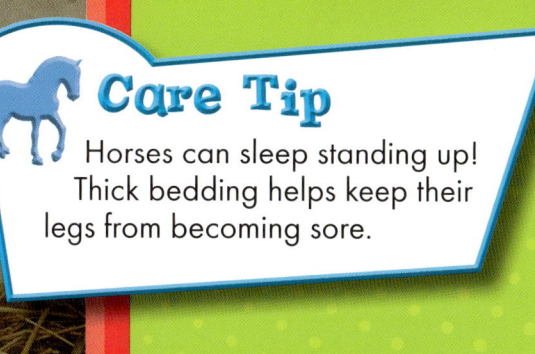

Care Tip
Horses can sleep standing up! Thick bedding helps keep their legs from becoming sore.

Feeding Your Horse

fun fact

A horse eats about 20 pounds (9 kilograms) of hay and drinks about 12 gallons (45 liters) of water every day.

Your horse needs a healthy diet. Put out hay in the morning and at night. Let your horse graze on grass. Give it grain or horse feed twice a day. Apple and carrot pieces are good treats!

Horses lose salt when they sweat. Set out a **salt block** for your horse to lick. Make sure your horse always has plenty of fresh, clean water.

← salt block

Grooming and Health

fun fact

Horses wear metal shoes to protect their hooves when they run. Nails hold the shoes to the hooves.

Groom your horse daily to keep it healthy. Brush your horse to remove dirt. Then wipe your horse down with a soft cloth. Use a **hoof pick** to remove dirt and stones from its hooves.

Your horse might need sheets or blankets. A horse blanket helps your horse stay warm in winter. In summer, a horse sheet protects your horse's body from biting flies.

horse blanket

Your horse needs to see a veterinarian twice a year. The veterinarian will check your horse's health and give it shots to prevent diseases.

Check your horse every day for changes in its health and habits. Look closely for sores or swelling on its legs. Your horse might be sick if it stops eating or is less active than usual.

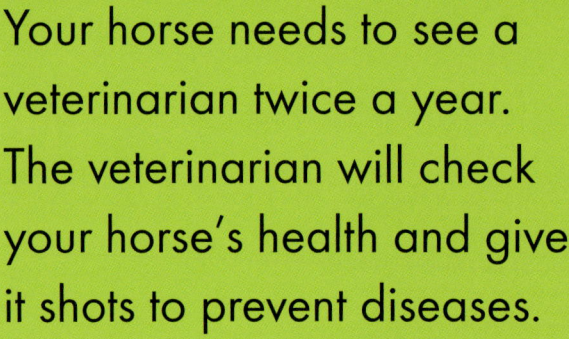

Care Tip

It is normal for horses to roll on the ground. They do this to stretch out their spines and their back muscles.

Exercising Your Horse

Horses need exercise every day. **Longeing** is one way to exercise your horse. Hook one end of a rope to your horse and hold the other end. Have your horse walk in a circle around you.

Riding your horse is the best exercise for it. Riding it a few times a week will help keep it healthy and happy. Giddyup!

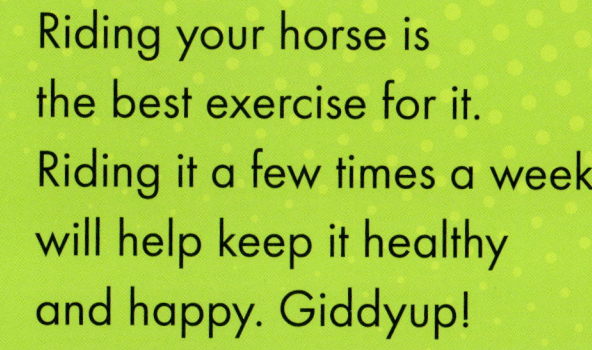

Glossary

bedding—material laid down as a bed for an animal

board—to pay someone to feed, shelter, and care for a horse

breeds—types of horses

groom—to clean

hoof pick—a metal tool used to remove dirt and stones from a horse's foot

horse trainer—someone who trains horses and advises horse owners on proper care

longeing—a way to exercise and train a horse in which a horse hooked to a rope walks in a circle around a handler

manure—animal waste

muck—to remove manure and soiled bedding from a horse's stall or shelter

pasture—a large, outdoor, fenced-in area; a pasture is a place for your horse to graze and move around.

salt block—a hard block of salt and other minerals that horses lick

stable—a place with one or more buildings where horses are kept

stall—a box-shaped area in a stable where a horse lives

temperament—the way a horse usually acts

veterinarian—a doctor who takes care of animals

To Learn More

AT THE LIBRARY
Draper, Judith. *My First Horse and Pony Care Book*. Boston, Mass.: Kingfisher, 2006.

O'Neal, Claire. *Care for a Pet Horse*. Hockessin, Del.: Mitchell Lane Publishers, 2009.

Stockland, Patricia M. *In the Horse Stall*. Edina, Minn.: Magic Wagon, 2008.

ON THE WEB
Learning more about pet care is as easy as 1, 2, 3.

1. Go to www.factsurfer.com.

2. Enter "pet care" into the search box.

3. Click the "Surf" button and you will see a list of related Web sites.

With factsurfer.com, finding more information is just a click away.

Index

bedding, 13
boarding, 8
breeds, 6, 7
exercise, 9, 20, 21
feeding, 8, 14, 15
grazing, 14
grooming, 16
hoof pick, 16
horse blanket, 17
horse sheet, 17
horse trainer, 7
life span, 5
longeing, 20
manure, 13
mucking, 13
pasture, 11
pet supplies, 5, 7, 9
riding, 6, 21
salt block, 15
sickness, 18

stable, 8
stall, 10, 13
temperament, 6
veterinarian, 7, 18

The images in this book are reproduced through the courtesy of: Eline Spek, front cover; Terrie L. Zeller, front cover (small); Diana Hirsch, pp. 4-5; Barry Blackburn, p. 5 (top); Michael Westhoff, p. 5 (middle); Ad van Brunschot, p. 5 (bottom); Juan Martinez, pp. 6 (top, middle, bottom), 8, 10 (small); Sonya Etchison, pp. 6-7; Imagesource/Photolibrary, p. 9; Teri & Jackie Soares, pp. 10-11; Juniors Bildarchiv/Alamy, pp. 12-13; Pixland/Photolibrary, pp. 14, 16; Juniors Bildarchiv/Photolibrary, p. 15; R H Productions/Photolibrary, p. 16 (small); Bencha Stewart, p. 17; Alexia Khruscheva, p. 18 (small); Michael Peuckert/Photolibrary, pp. 18-19; Juniors Bildarchiv, pp. 20-21; Elena Elisseeva, p. 21 (small).